Original title:

Melt Happens

Copyright © 2024 Creative Arts Management OÜ
All rights reserved.

Author: Theodore Sinclair
ISBN HARDBACK: 978-9916-94-198-0
ISBN PAPERBACK: 978-9916-94-199-7

The Gentle Embrace of Change

A snowman sighed, his hat askew,
As sunshine teased him, bright and new.
He danced away with a floppy grin,
While puddles formed where he had been.

A carrot nose, now adrift,
Bids farewell with a playful lift.
Children laugh as he winks goodbye,
Their laughter echoes beneath the sky.

A Symphony of Dripping Dreams

Icicles cling, a fragile ballet,
Performing tricks as they dream away.
Each drop a note in a sunny tune,
While rooftops gleam beneath the moon.

A symphony sweet of water and light,
As winter waves its last goodbye night.
They jive and jiggle, oh, what a spree,
A raucous party, just wait and see!

Where Ice Becomes Memory

In the fridge, a party of frost,
Each ice cube whispers of summers lost.
They wave their hands, full of cheer,
While the fridge hums old songs we hold dear.

Memories frozen in cold embrace,
Now warm and eager to find their place.
With smiles they slip from their icy tomb,
As laughter fills the melting room.

The Dappled Glow of Surrender

Sunshine tickles the frozen ground,
While winter's cloak makes a gentle sound.
Puddles form in a playful race,
Reflecting joy upon each face.

The world gives way, a vibrant show,
As streams begin their lively flow.
A melting heart, a funny fate,
Embracing change, we celebrate!

The Dance of Dew and Sunlight

In morning's grace, the dew prances,
Winking at rays with bold advances.
Each droplet giggles, a tiny show,
As sunlight tickles, making them glow.

A tap dance on leaves, a shimmering spree,
Nature's own party, just wait and see.
With blades of grass in a waltz, they play,
Spinning in circles, then fading away.

Softening Shadows of a Fading Chill

Chill hides in corners, trying to linger,
But warmth sneaks in, a sly little singer.
Shadows grow lazy, with a yawn and a stretch,
While chilly whispers find a new sketch.

Snowmen chuckle, starting to droop,
As sunlight dances, part of the troupe.
The frosty tale has not gone quite yet,
But warm hugs are coming, you can bet!

Transition: From Crystals to Currents

The frost on the window starts to behave,
With each sunny ray, a newer wave.
Crystals are giggling, unable to hold,
While puddles gather stories untold.

Once proud and rigid, now free to roam,
Those icy shards have found a new home.
In laughter and splashes, they rush right out,
No longer stiff, they're dancing about.

Erosion of the Frosted Veil

A veil of frost blushes in the heat,
Swaying and swishing, it admits defeat.
It giggles and sighs, 'Goodbye to this freeze,'
With each sunbeam, floating like a tease.

Down by the brook, the laughter flows,
Where chilly whispers now murmur and chose.
The frozen coat slips, brushing the ground,
And soon the whole world joins in the sound.

Thawing Echoes in the Breeze

The snowman takes a coffee break,
He sips with gusto, like a pro.
His carrot nose begins to shake,
As warmth puts on its silly show.

The ice cream truck rolls down the street,
With jingles loud enough to cheer.
But puddles form beneath our feet,
And squishy socks are drawing near.

Where Frost Gives Way

Beneath the frost, a party waits,
The squirrels wear shades, sipping tea.
They dance on branches, like lightweights,
While bunnies plot to steal some glee.

The garden starts to shed its chill,
Tulips poke heads, ready to shout.
A worm does flips; what a thrill!
He burrows out and gives a pout.

The Drip of Time

A single droplet swings and sways,
From icicle, it makes its drop.
Time drips slowly, through the days,
Like melted butter on a mop.

The gutter sings a happy tune,
As raindrops join in harmony.
The sun peeks out, a smiling moon,
And leaves invite the bees to swing.

Transformations in the Sunlight

A marshmallow campfire shrinks,
As laughter fills the open air.
The shadows dance, and no one thinks,
Of winter's chill or icy stare.

The ice cubes play a silly game,
As drinks are poured and fizzed to cheer.
They dive and jump, then start to blame,
Each other for that splashy smear!

Whispers of the Unfrozen

In a land of frosty giggles,
Where icicles hang like jiggly wobbles,
Snowmen rehearse their chilled ballet,
While penguins plot a jazzy getaway.

Chattering teeth and icy grins,
A parade of frozen furry sins,
Snowball fights that rattle the chest,
As winter's grip turns into jest.

Liquid Light Dancing

Sunlight spills like melted cheese,
On puddles where the children tease,
Jumping high, they splash and squeal,
As colors swirl in a slippery reel.

Rainbows twirl on pavement slick,
Duck and cover, dodging quick,
The sky laughs and begins to drop,
As laughter rises, never to stop.

The Tide of Transformation

The clock strikes noon with a bubbly cheer,
As the sun reveals a world so dear,
Beneath the weight of whimsical splashes,
Grass giggles as the last frost crashes.

A dance-off starts with a thundering clap,
As critters join with a silly flap,
The turtlenecks shrink, the shorts appear,
With sunglasses planted, summer's near.

Fragments of a Melting Heart

Once a fortress of icy pride,
Now a squishy pool, what a wild ride!
Chocolates left forgotten in the sun,
Melt with laughter, this isn't just fun.

A heart that wobbles with each new day,
Sways to the rhythm of a breezy ballet,
Embracing joy in a gooey embrace,
As love's warmth drips from every space.

When Frost Meets the Embrace of Day

The sun rises high, with a cheeky grin,
Frosty companions start to lose their skin.
A dance on the grass, they shiver and slide,
As warmth tiptoes in, they giggle and hide.

The icicles dangle, they jingle with glee,
Shouting, "Catch us if you can, look at me!"
But with each sunny beam, they shrink and they fade,
Like silly old jesters in the grand parade.

Puddles emerge, reflecting the cheer,
"Splish splash!" says the puddle, "I'm glad to be here!"
The flowers all poke their heads out to play,
Chuckling at frost's foolish getaway.

In this grand circus of warmth taking charge,
Frost trips and falls, but oh, it's so large!
With a wink to the sun and a nod to the grass,
Frost waves goodbye as the moments all pass.

The Language of Unraveling

In a world of wool and knit,
Scarves slip and hats will split.
A sneeze in spring, a giggle too,
Threads of joy in a warm breeze blew.

Laughter rolls as mittens fall,
A dance of snowflakes, one and all.
Fingers cold, but spirits bright,
We chase our dreams in giddy flight.

Nature's Release

The sun peeks in, with cheeky grins,
Chasing shadows, tickling chins.
With every ray, the ice gives way,
Nature chuckles, come out and play.

Puddles form where snow once lay,
Rubber boots cause a splashy fray.
Slips and giggles, a playful retreat,
Who knew winter could taste so sweet?

A Tapestry of Warmth

Grandma's quilt, so warm and wide,
Holds stories and warmth from inside.
Stitches of laughter, patches of cheer,
Every thread whispers, spring is near.

Hot cocoa spills, makes a messy art,
As marshmallows drift, they steal the heart.
In this cozy chaos, we find a way,
To savor moments, come what may.

The Last Whisper of Winter

Frosted breath, a playful tease,
As winter giggles with the breeze.
The final flake, a shy one lingers,
But springtime's here, it waves with fingers.

A snowman frowns, his hat askew,
He wobbles, laughs, bids us adieu.
With every sunbeam, warmth unfurls,
Nature knows how to twirl and whirl.

The Liquid Touch of Change

When ice cubes start to giggle,
And puddles form a wiggle,
A splash of warmth, oh what a sight,
The fridge's sigh, it's not quite right.

The frosty friends begin to fade,
They dance away, a slippery parade,
A sunbeam's wink, a playful tease,
Watch as they drip with the greatest ease.

A Symphony of Dissolving Chill

The orchestra of thawing ice,
Makes symphonies that sound so nice,
A conductor made of heat and sun,
As chilly notes begin to run.

With every drop, a note is played,
The concert hall becomes a trade,
Of splishy-splashy, merry cheers,
As winter's grip disappears.

Chasing the Last Crystals

Oh tiny flakes, you're almost gone,
A final chase, let's sing this song,
A frosty dash, a giggle here,
We'll catch you soon, don't disappear!

With twirling joy, we run around,
Hoping that you'll still be found,
But watch you dance, and then you slip,
And off you go on a sunny trip.

The Great Unraveling of Cold

In corners of the icy room,
Cold whispers start to meet their doom,
The laundry spins in chilly haste,
As warm embraces leave a taste.

The snowflakes laugh, a light-hearted chat,
Sinking lower in their floppy hat,
As frosty dreams begin to flail,
A comical and slippery tale.

Shimmering Raindrop Reverie

A droplet fell with a giggle,
It danced on a leaf, a sprightly wiggle.
Drip-drip, it slips off the edge,
Splashing down in a water hedge.

It tickled the grass, a playful tease,
Whispered to flowers, "Please don't freeze!"
Together they laughed at the chilly sway,
As sunshine waved goodbye to gray.

The Softening of Icebound Dreams

Once frozen thoughts lay on the ground,
Now they chuckle, unbound, unbound.
With each warm hour they begin to sway,
Silly visions, melting away.

A snowman sighs, his carrot nose droops,
"How I long to join the water loops!"
Puddles form with a splash and a wink,
Sharing secrets that sunbeams think.

When Warmth Begins to Weep

The sun wakes up with a yawn and a stretch,
Chasing old frost with a playful fetch.
"Come on, my friend, there's warmth to explore,"
As icicles giggle and slide to the floor.

Stumbling around, they roll in delight,
As puddles splash under bright morning light.
A chorus of water sings soft and sweet,
In this wacky world of the springtime beat.

Unraveling of Winter's Embrace

Winter's blanket gets tied in a knot,
As goofy heat dances, connects the dot.
With every wiggle, it starts to unwind,
The chilly retreat feels so far behind.

Snowflakes tumble like giggling sprites,
Falling apart in their playful fights.
"Catch me if you can!" they gleefully cry,
As warmth claims the ground beneath the sky.

The Release of Winter's Hold

Snowmen sit with a sigh,
Droopy hats and melted eye.
Icicles drip like a slow tune,
While penguins complain to the moon.

Winter's breath takes a break,
Even frost needs a good shake.
Gloves left lost, socks gone amiss,
Who knew frostbite would feel like bliss?

Hot cocoa spills on the floor,
Cup tipped over, what a chore!
Carrots turn to mushy bites,
While snowballs fade out of sights.

Everything starts to feel warm,
Winter's chill is losing form.
Patience thaws, and giggles rise,
As sunshine dances in the skies.

Streams of Unveiled Souls

Waterways chuckle and shout,
Freed from the ice, oh what a route!
Fish in disco, swimming free,
Splashing joy in jubilee.

Turtles throw their shells aside,
Stretched out basking, full of pride.
Echoes of laughter, birds take flight,
As the world stirs in morning light.

Rafts of twigs float in parade,
Waving hello, in the glade.
What a scene—it's pure delight,
As trees shake off their frosty bite.

Bridges made of melted dreams,
Water rushes, life redeems.
The thaw awakes all that's true,
Waving joy in every hue.

The Embrace of Forgotten Frost

Frosty whispers start to fade,
Socks and mittens form a raid.
Hats tumble down with a laugh,
As moments melt into the past.

Frosted windows, now a haze,
Dance of sunlight in a daze.
Snowflakes turn to giggles light,
No more chill, just pure delight.

Old ice skates find a home,
In the closet's dust to roam.
Skating dreams turn to puddles,
As laughter echoes through the cuddles.

We bid goodbye to frosty shivers,
Holding on to warm quivers.
As seasons change, here's the deal—
All things warm, let's make a meal!

Flowing into New Horizons

The sun peeks up with a grin,
Kissing frost where joys begin.
Rivers dance with a cheerful flow,
Painting the world in a glow.

Trails open wide, boots untied,
A joyful spill, can't hide my pride.
Slipping here, a comical fall,
Giggles echo, best of all.

Picnics planned with sandwiches bright,
Warmed by sun, what a sight!
The grass yawns, shakes off its night,
As new beginnings feel just right.

So here's to change, it's ray of cheer,
Waving goodbye to winter's sneer.
With open arms and happy hearts,
Adventure awaits, let's make a start!

Drifting Away from Rigidity

In winter's grip, I stood so tight,
Like a statue taking flight.
Yet warmth creeps in with a silly grin,
Now I'm swaying like a feathered fin.

I used to be a stiff old fool,
Chained to rules, like a stubborn mule.
But laughter bubbled, melted away,
Now I dance at dusk, come what may.

The Fluidity of Remembrance

Memories slip like water through hands,
Turning rigid walls into sandy lands.
I chuckle at thoughts that used to weigh,
Now they flow and frolic, come what may.

In the river of time, I float and glide,
With each silly lesson, I take in stride.
The past is a puddle, not a heavy load,
And I laugh as I dance down this winding road.

Embracing the Warmth of Dusk

As day recedes and shadows play,
I wiggle and giggle in a silly way.
Golden beams turn serious frowns,
Into soft giggles and gentle crowns.

With every glow, I wiggle my toes,
In the twilight laughter, anything goes.
The sky blushes pink, and I join the cheer,
With a chuckle or two, I have nothing to fear.

Shadows of a Thawing Heart

My heart was a rock, oh so cold,
Anchored to fears, stories untold.
But gentle warmth crept quietly near,
Dancing around and tickling my fear.

With each thawing hour, I giggle and glow,
Finding joy in the slip and flow.
Shadows of worry begin to depart,
As laughter emerges from a thawing heart.

A Song of Soft Defiance

Snowmen cry with joyous glee,
As puddles form beneath their knee.
With carrot noses washed away,
They dance in boots, come join the play.

Icicles hang like frozen spears,
But sunshine cheers, it's time for beers.
They quiver, drip, a soft salute,
To warmer days in weather's suit.

The snowflakes grin, their work undone,
While children cheer, let's go have fun!
A slide, a splash, all joy and cheer,
Embrace the silly, hold it dear.

So grab a cup, let's make a toast,
To thawing friends we love the most.
With laughter shared, we take our stand,
In nature's game, we all can band.

Melodies of the Thaw

Drips and drops are falling free,
A symphony of jubilee.
The winter's grip begins to sway,
As giggles chase the chill away.

A puddle forms, it shines like glass,
And kids in boots all run and splash.
The sun ignites the snowy fields,
With warmth that nature gently yields.

Snowball fights turn into soups,
As kids transform to goofball groups.
They make a mess, their laughter loud,
Umbrellas bloom, they feel so proud.

So as we wander, hearts set free,
Let's sing of joy and jubilee.
With warmth and fun, let's take the lead,
In this wild dance of spring's sweet seed.

The Driftwood of Time

Time rolls by like coffee sips,
With laughter shared—no time for slips.
We grab the past, a silly ride,
As driftwood floats on joyful tide.

Each warm ray teases winter's grip,
And socks now dry are on a trip.
With colors bright, the world awakes,
And all the plastic flamingos quake.

Puddles form, a funny sight,
As ducks parade, they feel just right.
With wiggly feet and handy spins,
We twirl around, let fun begin!

So gather 'round, don't be shy,
Let's sing beneath a sunny sky.
In this wild warp of fleeting time,
We laugh and play, oh how sublime!

Holding the Essence of the Warmth

A t-shirt worn on winter's breath,
The chill may come, but joy won't rest.
With blankets tossed, we laugh and tease,
As sunlight spreads with such great ease.

Cocoa spills, a tasty fluke,
While snowflakes melt, and dance like Duke.
A summer wish in frozen shoes,
Brings warmer smiles, we can't refuse.

With flip-flops on in snowy scenes,
The fun unfolds, a life of dreams.
With wavy hair and carefree hearts,
This playful shift is just the start.

So let's embrace this lovely split,
And hold the warmth, we can't quit.
From winter's chill to spring's soft charm,
We laugh aloud, with open arms.

A Canvas of Change

The ice was thick like grandma's stew,
But then the sun just laughed and flew.
Colors splashed where white had been,
A slippery dance in the wake of a grin.

Puddles formed like little lakes,
I saw a duck doing double takes.
Sleds lost their charm, now just a tease,
As we giggled, shaking off the freeze.

Snowmen drooped with a sighing face,
Wishing they could join the race.
They whispered tales of wintry cheer,
While we splashed puddles, shedding our fear.

So let's embrace this funny plight,
Where snowballs fade in the morning light.
A canvas bright where winter laugh,
Painting joy in its aftermath.

The Lightness of Being Unfrozen

I woke up to a world askew,
Where my fridge was my ice-cream crew.
A soda can rolled with a cheer,
As yogurt danced, shedding its fear.

The icicles started to perform,
Like a frozen flash mob, the new norm.
They swung and swayed to the spring's best beat,
As the sun cheered, "Get on your feet!"

We chased our shadows in the bright day,
While frostbite memories slipped away.
A snowflake hat declared a truce,
Spinning that's given a new excuse.

Now each puddle holds a deep joke,
As ice cream cones no longer choke.
Laughter rings with warmth so bold,
A sweet release from winter's hold.

Whispers of the Thaw

Once a fortress of icy pride,
Now a slide, where giggles glide.
The chill retreats on tippy toes,
As secrets spill where the sunshine glows.

Frosty faces flicker and fade,
As melted beams start a parade.
A waffle cone met a sunny breeze,
And giggled loud, "I'm done with freeze!"

The winter gloves now flirt with sun,
As they roll away, finally done.
The scarf's a banner of freedom's claim,
While we all cheer — it's not the same!

So raise your voice to the warming air,
Join the dance, you've nothing to spare.
Laughter bubbles, it's time to draw,
The playful whispers that break the thaw.

Drip by Drip

Droplets dance from the roof,
As sunshine warms the ground,
A puddle forms, what a goof,
Nature's laughter all around.

Each tear from ice, a giggly plop,
Creating ripples, they bounce and play,
From chilly peaks to a bubbly drop,
Making the snowmen rue the day.

The Heart Unfurls

Like a flower in springtime's grace,
The cold retreats with a chuckle,
A heart made warm in a sunny embrace,
Who knew ice could be so fickle?

Crispy edges begin to fade,
With every beam, a shy reveal,
From stark and bright to a lovely shade,
Life's a jest in the warmth we feel.

Frost's Farewell: A Gentle Surrender

Goodbye to frosty heebie-jeebies,
As warmth brings giggles from the trees,
The icy grip softens with ease,
Nature's prank played as it pleases.

With every ray that stakes its claim,
What once was fierce, now takes the blame,
For all the shivers, and silly shame,
As temperatures rise, it's a joyful game.

Fractured Snowflakes in the Sun

Snowflakes, once proud, now stroll in beams,
With fractured forms, they laugh and tease,
Like playful children, devouring dreams,
Turning solid joys into breezy pleas.

They swirl and giggle, then fade away,
Dropping zany shapes in cozy pools,
A chilly dance turned bright and gay,
Playing tricks, they break the rules.

Embrace of the Liquid Dawn

When morning breaks, a splashy cheer,
The world wakes up with a silly grin,
Waters twirl, no hint of fear,
In liquid light, the fun begins.

Kisses from the sun, they tumble down,
Transforming frost into pure delight,
With every drop, the earth's new gown,
It's a party where cold turns light.

Drifting Towards Freedom

In a world where ice cream bows,
Squirrels dance in absurd throws.
Lollipops spin on melting feet,
We laugh at puddles, oh what a feat!

Chocolate dreams in the sun's embrace,
Balloons slip past, a silly race.
Flavors collide with giggling glee,
As we chase joy, whatever it be!

Sunhats fly, a wondrous sight,
Caught in the breeze, they take flight.
Wobbly cones, a comical plight,
We chase the sweetness, oh what light!

Slipping on treats, we give a cheer,
Popcorn fluff, our snack frontier.
With each splat, we find delight,
On this journey, oh what a sight!

In the Shadows of Warmth

Under blankets that cuddle tight,
A grumpy snowman bemoans his plight.
With a sigh, he gazes wide,
At the melting sun where dreams abide.

He tells tales of snowy days,
While the sun laughs and plays.
Tears of ice drip with glee,
As snowflakes join in a quirky spree!

Popsicles wink from their cool perch,
While warm winds tease, it's an odd search.
Laughter erupts from slippery lands,
As snowmen noodle in awkward strands.

Down the slide of warmth and cheer,
We greet each splash without a fear.
In the shadows, giggles soar,
In this world of warmth, we want more!

The Nudging of Boundaries

A snowball fight turned pizza pie,
Who knew ice could say goodbye?
With frozen noses, grins galore,
We venture forth, forever more!

Ice cubes tango on the floor,
While lemonade clouds float and soar.
As pickles giggle in a jar,
We redefine just how bizarre!

Wobbly tables, silly chairs,
Each bounce invites a playful dare.
With every slip on smeared-up dreams,
We scribble joy in hearty beams.

So let's nudge the boundaries away,
With laughter guiding our sprightly play.
In this ruckus, we'll find the rhyme,
Making silly memories through time!

Awakening from a Frosty Slumber

As winter waves its sleepy hand,
Flowers giggle, take a stand.
The frost begins its grand retreat,
As bunnies bounce on carefree feet.

Frosty teapots whistle loud,
While coffee spills from a jolly crowd.
With each step on the frosty ground,
We hear the joyous sounds abound!

Skates turn into rollerblades,
As chilly ghosts flee the glades.
The sun cracks jokes on frosty flakes,
While silly songs fill up the lakes.

Awake from dreams, we shake it free,
With every giggle, we splash with glee.
In this thaw, let's dance anew,
With warmer hearts and skies so blue!

When the Ground Breathes Free

The ground starts to grin, oh what a sight,
Cracks and pops, a true delight.
Puddles form, little lakes appear,
Splashing about brings us cheer.

Grass shoots up, doing a jig,
Nature's dance, so bold and big.
We skip and slide on muddy floors,
Who knew the earth had such open doors?

Bees buzz low, they swarm around,
Finding joy where chaos is found.
Chasing puddles, we laugh with glee,
The ground breathes free, oh my, whee!

It's a playful twist, life's little game,
Suddenly, we're never the same.
With every step, a new surprise,
The earth has tricks, oh my, look at those skies!

Ebb and Flow of Change

Waves roll in with bouncing waves,
The shoreline laughs, oh how it misbehaves.
Sandcastles rise, then tumble down,
If the tide's a joker, it wears a crown.

Seagulls caw, they dive and sway,
Watching chaos in grand ballet.
With each retreat, we squeal and run,
Where's the beach, just having fun?

Footprints drawn, but they won't stay,
Like secrets lost, they slip away.
We giggle loud at each surprise,
As water hugs and bids goodbye.

Oh, life's a dance, a merry jest,
With ebb and flow, we're always blessed.
Chasing waves, full of laughter,
In this funny game, we find our rafter!

Softening of the Steel Grip

The winter holds on, but oh how it tires,
A shiver and squeak, as it quietly tires.
Old frosty frowns begin to fade,
And grumpy old snowmen finally wade.

Breezes blow soft, tickling our ears,
Out come the jokes, and so do the cheers.
With each ray of sun, the chill takes a bow,
Waving goodbye to the frostbitten vow.

Umbrellas close; the rain starts to play,
Rubber boots dance, oh what a display!
Puddles form and splashes roar,
Life's once again, a yelp out the door!

Our coats shed off, with laughter in tow,
Ready to greet the warmth with a glow.
When winter is fickle, we take a look,
And write all our giggles in a fun nature book!

Radiance of Evolving Moments

With each tick of time, the sun draws near,
Moments arise, each full of cheer.
Laughter bursts forth, like bubbles of air,
Such radiant joy, it isn't rare.

Clouds drift away, like lost little dreams,
Sunbeams peek out, the merriment beams.
Every tick, every tock, a laugh we claim,
In the game of life, it's all just the same.

As clocks unspool, giggles ignite,
The thrill of change feels oh-so-right.
We dance to the rhythm of time's gentle flow,
In this bright existence, together we glow.

So chase each moment, don't let them fray,
In the fabric of life, find your own play.
With radiant smiles, we carve our way,
Embracing the fun in every day!

Erosion of Winter's Edge

Snowmen build as if they're proud,
With carrot noses, standing loud.
But spring winks with a sunny grin,
And soon the trouble will begin.

Icicles dangle, sharp and blue,
They wave goodbye, it's time to stew.
With laughter, winter's reign grows thin,
As puddles form, a soft chagrin.

Sleds now rest where grass appears,
While laughter echoes, no more fears.
Oh, winter's throne, you've lost your touch,
As chubby cheeks begin to clutch.

But don't you worry, winter dear,
You'll be back, we all will cheer.
For every season takes a turn,
And with each thaw, we live and learn.

Song of the Sunlit Tides

Beaches beckon with a laugh,
As waves break forth, they dance and chaff.
The sun performs its nightly chore,
While seagulls squawk and dive for more.

Flip-flops flap, a joyful sound,
While ice cream melts into the ground.
With every drip, a giggle spreads,
As sticky hands scratch sandy heads.

The shoreline giggles, what a sight,
Where swimsuits cling with all their might.
As tides pull back and forth in glee,
The sun invites all hearts to free.

So show your toes, let worries go,
As laughter dances with each flow.
For even summer knows it's true,
That joy will come, no matter if you stew.

When Rigid Meets Radiant

In a land where ice is king,
Froze in time, no hope of spring.
But suddenly, the sun did tease,
And rigid hearts began to freeze.

The penguins waddle, slip and slide,
While rays of warmth they cannot hide.
With melting hopes and thrills to chase,
They find a puddle, sweet embrace.

Watch the frosty friends collide,
With hugs of warmth, can't run or hide.
A ticklish splash, and suddenly,
They're swimming in absurdity.

So here's to all those icy times,
When fun is found in silly crimes.
Let rigid hearts learn to rejoice,
For warmth may lead to a funny voice.

The Sweet Surrender of Ice

Once a fortress, proud and bold,
Now surrendering to warmth untold.
With cheerful giggles, the ice does sigh,
As it slips away, oh my, oh my!

The frosties laugh, they ebb and flow,
As sunshine kisses all below.
A dance of droplets, what a sight,
While puddles form, hearts feel delight.

Snowflakes whisper of their fate,
With frosty giggles, they congregate.
For every shimmer, there's a cheer,
As winter waves its time, oh dear.

So raise a glass, or just a cup,
To toast the ice that's melting up.
For sweet surrenders can be fun,
In every drop, a new day's sun.

Awakening: The Drip of Time

In the quiet morn, a drip sings low,
Puddles form where snowdrifts used to glow.
A squirrel slips and does a funny dance,
Nature chuckles at its own frosty chance.

Drips turn to streams, a gushing complaint,
Icicles drip-drop, a laughter quaint.
Bunnies hop, their tails wagging in glee,
As old man Winter sips his tea.

With each little drip, the world starts to play,
Skipping and laughing, it's a whimsical day.
Raindrops wear hats, fashionably new,
Making puddle reflectors just for you!

So gather the drops with your silly grin,
As the sun winks mischievously from within.
Let giggles abound, let mirth find its way,
For time's funny drips are here to stay.

Sunlit Moments in Quiet Thaws

The sunshine sneaks in with a smirk so sly,
Tickling the frost as it waves goodbye.
A robin croons from a branch up high,
While the daisies yawn and start to pry.

Warmth tickles noses, a slap on the cheek,
Ice cubes giggle, lending blunders unique.
But watch your step, oh, don't take a fall,
On slippery patches, the laughs come to call!

With sunshine's warmth, the world starts to sway,
Puddles become mirrors for children at play.
Splashes of laughter, oh what a delight,
As tiny feet jump and soar in mid-flight!

In these sunlit moments, joy blooms like a flower,
Each drop is a jester, each ray a tower.
So dance with the drip, and sway with the thaw,
For laughter will bloom, that's the grand law!

Seasons in Transition: A Poetic Flow

Frost bids farewell with a wink and a grin,
As buds start to giggle and warmth seeps in.
Socks squelch in puddles, while children scream,
Springtime arrives with a playful gleam!

The garden awakens, oh what a sight,
With flowers in tutu, dazzlingly bright.
Bees buzzing by, doing a little jig,
While squirrels debate on how to dig.

Quick as a flash, the seasons will swap,
A flip of a switch—the world goes pop!
Leaves flip and swirl, like a waltzing show,
While nature chuckles, just letting it flow.

Yearning for bliss, in this cycle we twirl,
Seasons with giggles, each twist a whirl.
Join in the fun, let the laughter ignite,
In this zany dance of day and night!

The Soliloquy of Water's Embrace

Oh, hear the whispers of water's soft cheer,
In every puddle, joy gathers near.
A mischievous drop, its journey begun,
Trickles from rooftops, laughter like fun.

Mops and brooms join in the frolicsome spree,
Chasing the raindrops as they tumble with glee.
Little fish giggle beneath the bright wave,
While otters practice their best belly wave.

A splash in the park makes children all squeal,
Each ripple a tickle, oh, what a feel!
With umbrellas turned boats, they sail through the foam,
Every drop has a story, each splash finds a home.

So listen closely, to water's sweet tease,
As it twirls and jives in the playful breeze.
In comical dance, as they tumble and play,
In nature's embrace, hilarity stays!

Warm Breezes Upon Frozen Waters

A breeze that dances, quite absurd,
Makes frozen lakes sing like a bird.
Ice wobbling, giggling with delight,
Nature's laughter, quite a sight.

Chairs on the ice, we're ready to sit,
But alas, the ice gives a sly little split.
We tumble and splash, what a funny scene,
Who knew winter could be so keen?

The snowmen tremble, shaking with glee,
As they're worried their hats might just flee.
While squirrels chip in, playing their tricks,
We're laughing out loud, getting our kicks.

So here we are, with puddles galore,
Slipping and sliding, begging for more.
Life turns wacky, ain't it a hoot?
Warm breezes come, and our winter's a hoot!

Echoes of a Thawing Silence

Quiet whispers in the chill of the dawn,
Cracks and pops, it's winter's last yawn.
The ice is giggling, slipping away,
And we're ready to laugh at the play.

Snowflakes are scurrying off with a cheer,
While icicles drip, bringing our beer.
The chilly jokes that once ruled the scene,
Are thawing to laughter, fresh and clean.

With every step, we leave our old tracks,
The frozen past begins to relax.
Old frosty frowns turn to silly grins,
As the thawed echoes reveal all our sins.

So sing to the ice with a gleeful tune,
Let's embrace the sun, and dance with a loon.
We're waiting for spring, with a wink and a nudge,
As winter tips its hat, and we all give a judge.

In the Arms of the Guiding Sun

Under the rays, the ice starts to melt,
A squirrel chuckles, his fur lightly felt.
He tiptoes softly on the warm, wet ground,
While we're laughing at chaos all around.

Socks turned to squish from puddles galore,
As we chase after a dog on the floor.
Splashing and slipping, the giggles begin,
Emerging from winter, a joyful spin!

A snowball fight turns to a water spree,
With laughter erupting like bubbles from tea.
Oh, the silliness, we're all in a flurry,
While the sun shakes off winter with hurry.

So raise a toast to the guiding light,
To the fun-filled days that follow the night.
We'll bask in the warmth, our troubles now flown,
In the arms of sunshine, we've brightly shone.

From Icebound Chains to Gentle Streams

Chains of the cold begin to unwind,
While ducks in the pond deliver a find.
Chasing their tails on a flotilla of laughs,
As we watch the ice write its silly gaffs.

The cold grip loosens, the stage starts to warm,
A frosty old bear now starts to perform.
With a clumsy twist and a tumble so grand,
He's become the comedian, you understand?

Wiggling and giggling with glee in the sun,
Our hearts feel the jesting, it's all just pure fun.
From frozen to fluid, each heartbeat a stream,
We're swept in a whirlpool of laughter and dream.

So here's to the warmth and the chaos divine,
To nature's slapstick, and the elderly line.
From icebound chains, we'll break free with style,
With each silly moment, we'll cherish the while.

The Sweetness of Surrender

Chocolate dribbles down my chin, oh dear,
Caught in a moment that brings me cheer.
Each lick and bite is a sticky affair,
Yet no one can resist, we all want to share.

Sundaes wobble, they threaten to fall,
With sprinkles on top, they're a rainbow ball.
"Catch me if you can!" the desserts seem to shout,
As laughter erupts, without a doubt.

Whipped cream clouds float in the sun's embrace,
"Dive in, take a chance!" they grin, it's a race.
Drinks spill over, and the napkins flee,
In this gooey war, we're wild and free!

Every tasty moment, we savor with glee,
As the sugar rush takes over, whee!
With giggles aplenty, we give in to fate,
Surrendering sweetness, oh isn't it great?

Transience Beneath the Sun

Sands shift lightly, as shapes start to form,
The castles we build will face a warm storm.
The sun roars loudly, "Let's have some fun!"
Yet all know the truth; it's a game that's done.

Laughter tickles the salty sea breeze,
As kids run for cover, oh please, oh please!
The tides come in, with a giggling sound,
While the plastic shovels are lost and found.

Seagulls swoop down, with cheeky delight,
Thinking our snacks make an excellent bite.
Our sandwiches vanish, like hopes in a splash,
"Don't feed the birds!" But they're gone in a flash.

As the sun dips low, the colors ignite,
We cherish the chaos, it's pure paradise.
Transience lingers, but it's alright,
With sun-kissed memories, we hold on tight.

Transforming in the Arms of the Sun

In the morning glow, we start to sway,
With puddles forming, we're on our way.
Sun's warm embrace, a hug for the day,
Oh look! My ice cream's begun to play!

The more I giggle, the more I slide,
Across a bench or a sunny ride.
I swear I'm solid, where do I hide?
But laughter's too much; I'm oozing with pride!

I wave to the sun, "Hey buddy, not fair!"
Each ray a tickle, I'm losing my hair.
In a wobbly waltz, I dance with flair,
Come take a look! I'm almost a chair!

I'll tell you a secret, just me and you,
Being all liquid is such a fun view.
Life's just a splash, oh the joy, it's true,
In sticky situations, I'm thriving anew.

Threads of Liquid Joy

In a pot on the stove, I bubble with glee,
Twirling and whirling, all mixy and free.
Some say I'm soup, oh don't you agree?
But I'm more like a stream, just wait and see.

The noodles go in, oh what a sight!
They dance in the broth, what pure delight.
Gravity giggles at such a great height,
As I start to splatter, what a wild flight!

A sprinkle of spice and a dash of fun,
I'm a party in flavors, second to none.
Each slurp is a laugh, oh isn't it pun?
Who knew being liquid could make me a bun?

With each little swirl, I'm feeling so right,
Riding on waves of a culinary plight.
So grab me a bowl, let's celebrate tonight,
In threads of liquid joy, we'll unite!

Cascading Change

Watch out! Here comes a slippery show,
As ice cubes tumble, watch them go!
Rolling and bouncing, oh what a glow,
Can you catch me? I'm wiggly, though!

Down the hill, I take my flight,
Whoosh and giggle, a silly delight.
With every bounce, I feel so light,
Oh dear! Who knew I'd end the night?

A puddle here, a splash so grand,
Is this the lake where I take my stand?
Making new friends, just as I planned,
Together we flow, oh isn't it grand?

So cheer for the raindrops that fall from the sky,
They giggle and shimmer as they pass by.
In cascading change, we always comply,
For being in motion makes the heart fly.

The Cradle of Fluid Dreams

There's a wiggly world where we laugh and sway,
With jello-like wonders that puddle and play.
A cradle of dreams in a funky way,
Join the bounce party; we'll dance 'til May!

Each jiggle ignites a laugh or a cheer,
Swirling with joy as the sunset draws near.
Watch as we shimmer, crystal-clear,
It's a slippery fairytale, come gather near!

From spoons to sinks, we slide with grace,
With giggly glee and a splash on your face.
In the cradle of dreams, we'll found our space,
Where laughter and joy come to embrace!

So dip your toes in the fun, so bright,
As we merge with the magic, a twinkling sight.
In whirls of delight, we dance through the night,
In the cradle of fluid dreams, oh what a flight!

Softening Silhouettes

In winter's grasp, they start to sway,
Their edges blur, then slip away.
Puddles form where they once stood,
The sun laughs loud, it's all quite good.

Frosty friends just can't hold on,
To sunshine's charm, they're soon all gone.
The snowmen dance, they wobble and spin,
'Til they become a soggy grin.

Once sharp as ice, now soft as cream,
Life's a joke, or so it seems.
They chase their tails, like kids at play,
'Til they're just puddles at the end of day.

So let them giggle, laugh, and cheer,
For soggy fun is finally here.
Like ice cream cones in summer's glee,
All's well that drips, you see, you see!

When Ice Meets Flame

A frosty pickle on the range,
Meets a flame with a cheeky change.
They dance a jig, sizzle, and pop,
The icy dude can't handle the drop.

The stove laughs loud, it knows the game,
As ice cubes shout, 'This is so lame!'
They hiss and steam in a hot embrace,
A slippery showdown, what a case!

Drippy trails mark their wild flight,
As frosty dreams fade into the night.
From cool to warm, then boom! All gone,
Just sticky splatters to carry on.

So raise a glass to this wild fight,
Where ice and flame dance with delight.
Humor sizzles in each little drop,
In the kitchen, fun never can stop!

The Warmth of Whispered Change

Whispers float on the morning air,
Ice melts soft, what's fair isn't fair.
The sun tickles each chilly nook,
As shadows giggle, take a look.

Drips and drops start to take flight,
Like watercolors in golden light.
A frosty laugh, a gleeful cheer,
What once was hard is now so dear.

Siddling close, the sun and snow,
Trade silly jokes like friends that know.
They wink and grin with a cheeky charm,
Who knew a thaw could cause such harm?

So let us dance, with sticky feet,
In puddles where the warm sun greets.
For every splash and silly game,
Brings laughter that we won't reclaim!

Liquid Dreams Drift

In a glass jar, dreams take a ride,
Sailing down with nowhere to hide.
A splash here, a dribble there,
Oh, how wobbly dreams can fare!

They giggle and swirl like silly fish,
Each drop a wish, each splash a dish.
Gravity's humor plays its trick,
As visions slip and slip and slick.

Once hard and bright, now flowing free,
What once was chilled is pure jubilee.
Float on your dreams, they'll guide your way,
Through puddly paths where giggles play.

So raise a toast to laughing streams,
Where all is fun in liquid beams.
With every droplet's cheerful sway,
Life's a drizzle, come what may!

Foundations of Liquid Love

In a world where ice can sing,
Cupid's arrows, on ice, take wing.
Hearts slip and slide on snowy floors,
Love drips down like candy stores.

Sugar coatings, puddles of glee,
We dance around, so carelessly.
Swirling emotions, can't find their feet,
Love is messy, but oh so sweet!

When hearts are warm, they start to drip,
With giggles and laughter, we take a trip.
In sunlit laughter, we splash and play,
Turning cold nights into a sunny day.

Romance brews like tea, hot and bright,
While ducks do waddle, such a funny sight.
Love in each droplet, in each little plop,
We dive right into the ice cream shop!

Fluid Echoes of Transformation

In cups of warmth, our hearts awake,
As frosty flakes begin to shake.
The snowmen wave, they know the deal,
Tomorrow they'll be something surreal.

A slip and slide will rule the day,
With giggles masked, we glide away.
The winter's chill begins to tease,
As cozy thoughts take flight like bees.

The thaw makes way for splashes bright,
In puddles forming, we find delight.
Just grab your boots and jump on in,
As splashes of joy create a din!

Life's a melting pot, sticky and sweet,
We'll bubble over with laughter, not defeat.
Every drop sparkles, it's not a race,
In the chaos, we find our place!

The Heart's Response to Warmth

When sunbeams dance on frostbit grass,
Cold hearts begin to change, alas.
Awkward hugs make roly-poly friends,
In the warmth of laughter, love transcends.

Oh, quirky moments full of flair,
Like snowmen tripping without a care.
With silly faces, we let it out,
As warmth spreads love, there's no doubt.

The cold cannot keep our spirits low,
We laugh through the mishaps, our hearts aglow.
In puddles of warmth, we gather round,
In a melting embrace, true joy is found!

Hearts do wiggle, they twist and twirl,
With every giggle, they start to swirl.
As temperatures rise and smiles don their best,
We embrace this mess, it's life's funny jest.

Flowing with the Horizon

Under the horizon, where colors mix,
Life's just a play, a series of tricks.
The laughter flows like streams so bright,
With every chuckle, we take flight.

Chasing sunsets on slippery shores,
With flip-flop claps and ocean roars.
As waves come crashing, they giggle with glee,
Singing sweet songs, just you and me.

In the dance of the tides, we'll take a chance,
While the world around us starts to prance.
Every splash is a moment, ready to seize,
In a flow of delight, even the pretzels tease!

With salty air and joy in our hearts,
We laugh at the world and all its parts.
The horizon beckons, come join the fun,
As we float through life, like a water gun!

Unraveled Threads of Ice

Once a fortress, now a drip,
Noses catch a playful slip.
Snowmen frown at sunny beams,
While children chase their wilder dreams.

Polar bears in shorts parade,
While frosty art turns into jade.
Jack Frost lost the winning streak,
Now sunbathers spill their cheek.

Frozen lakes begin to sway,
Skaters glide, then come to play.
Ice cream dreams in every lick,
The spoon comes down, it feels like trick.

Nature giggles with its games,
Reminding us it's full of blames.
As winter bows, we shout with glee,
Who knew the warmth could set us free?

Cascades of Fleeting Time

Time drips quick like melting wax,
Clock hands dance with silly hacks.
The minutes slide right off the plate,
And who's the fool that stays out late?

Ice caps wink with a teasing grin,
As warmth spins tales of thick and thin.
Popsicles giggle, lost their chill,
While tropic birds fulfill the thrill.

Watch the glaciers shake and shimmy,
As silly seals flip and skimmy.
Not a care for chilly stays,
Just a splash in gold sun's rays.

Each tick feels like a fleeting race,
In this goofy, warm embrace.
Laughter echoes in the breeze,
As nature plays, and so we tease.

The Unbinding of Nature's Grasp

Socks and mittens hung so high,
As winter learns to wave goodbye.
Snowdrifts melt like candy dreams,
While laughter bubbles, or so it seems.

Icicles drip a symphony,
Nature hums in harmony.
Puddles giggle at each step,
Rainbow ducks around corners prep.

Old man winter's lost his snap,
Left his bag of frozen chap.
Flowers peep with a sunny shout,
Searching for what life's about.

Nature can't help but chortle loud,
As winter turns into the crowd.
Each slip and slide, a joyous theme,
In life's bright, whimsical meme.

Surrender to the Soothing Heat

Caught in sunbeams, all aglow,
Seeking shade from the fiery show.
Flip-flops flop with a happy tune,
Melting thoughts like a tasty croon.

Picnics sprout in grassy knolls,
While ants march out on fun-filled strolls.
Lemonade spills in laughter's lap,
A sticky joy in this sunny trap.

Watch the sun just have its fun,
As we complain but still we run.
Sweaty faces, but smiles so bright,
In this warm, eternal light.

As ice cream drips, we chase the bliss,
Each frozen treat, a playful kiss.
Under the sun, we dance like flowers,
Surrendering time to sunny hours.

The Transformation of Silence

In winter's chill, the quiet found,
A snowman grins, not making a sound.
But wait! What's this? A sly little thaw,
His carrot nose fell, oh what a flaw!

The ice cube's party, they slide and they sway,
On sunny days, they just can't stay.
With giggles and splashes, they splash in delight,
As puddles gather for a mini-water fight!

The snowflakes dance in a playful spree,
A warm breeze whispers, 'Just wait and see.'
As they puddle together, make quite a scene,
Who knew snow could be so keen?

So raise your glass to the warmth in the air,
And laugh with the ice that has vanished somewhere.
They're off to the ocean or maybe the bay,
While winter's speechless, they chuckle away!

When Icicles Weep in Light

Icicles hanging, sharp as a knife,
Glisten and glimmer, full of icy life.
But sunshine comes peeking, 'What's this I see?'
Drip, drop, dribble, oh, let it be!

Each tear they drop is a chuckle so sweet,
Feeling a bit soggy beneath summer's heat.
That tiny drip-drop orchestra plays in glee,
While water below claims, 'It's all about me!'

The rooftops tremble, oh what a sight!
As icicles shiver in the warm daylight.
There's laughter above, and splashes below,
A symphony of drips, in a sunshine show!

The sunlight reigns, what a comical feat,
As frosty warriors say, 'We've tasted defeat.'
They giggle and giggle, then slide away fast,
Leaving memories of winter that just couldn't last!

Spring's Quiet Erosion of Winter

Winter's the boss, holding tight with a frown,
Wearing his coat made of snowflakes and brown.
But wait! Here comes spring, a jester so sly,
With a wink and a nudge, makes him say bye-bye!

The ground starts to quake, with a wiggle and jig,
The snowmen shout, 'What's the deal, big wig?'
As daisies run wild, and the grass starts to grow,
The winter king mumbles, 'Can't we take it slow?'

A puddle reflects all the sunbeams that tease,
While winter's remorse seems to wheeze in the breeze.
The light-hearted blooms burst out in cheer,
Creating a scene that winter won't hear!

So tiptoe on flowers, rejoice in the cheer,
For the laughing winds holler, 'Winter, disappear!'
As the frosty old monarch walks off with a sigh,
Leaving behind just a cupcake or pie!

Tender Glimmers of a Warming Day

The sun stretches limbs, yawning wide in the sky,
As warm breezes whisper, `Oh I can't lie!`
It's time for the flowers to wake from their sleep,
As creatures peek out from the burrows so deep.

The squirrels are leaping, chasing their tails,
While the birds with their tunes tell epic tales.
Every tree shakes off its wintery coat,
With a giggle or two, puts on something remote!

Children giggle while puddles join in,
While skipping on sidewalks with laughter and spin.
As sweaters get tossed to the back of the drawer,
The warmth wraps around like a friendly encore.

So raise up your glasses to this beautiful day,
With sunshine and laughter to sweep gloom away.
Let's celebrate warmth with a melody played,
In honor of all those who dared to invade!

Milton Keynes UK
Ingram Content Group UK Ltd.
UKHW031319271124
451618UK00007B/224